Protection Program Defensive Planning For Fixed Facilities

This Page Intentionally Left Blank

TABLE OF CONTENTS

TABLE OF FIGURES

FOREWORD

This Department of Energy Technical Standard is for use by all Departmental elements. Beneficial comments (recommendations, additions, and deletions) and any pertinent data that may improve this document should be emailed to richard.faiver@hq.doe.gov or mailed to:

U.S. Department of Energy
Office of Health, Safety, and Security
Office of Security Policy, GTN/HS-51
1000 Independence Ave., SW
Washington, D.C. 20585-1290

Department of Energy Technical Standards do not establish requirements. However, all or part of the provisions in this Technical Standard can become requirements under the following circumstances:

- They are explicitly stated to be requirements in a Department of Energy requirements document (e.g., a purchase requisition).

- The organization makes a commitment to meet a standard in a contract, implementation plan, or program plan.

- This Technical Standard is incorporated into a contract.

Throughout this Technical Standard, the word "shall" is used to denote actions that must be performed if the objectives of this Standard are to be met. If the provisions in this Technical Standard are made requirements through one of the three ways discussed above, then the "shall" statements would become requirements.

Goals or intended functionality are indicated by "may," or "should." It is not appropriate to consider that "should" statements would automatically be converted to "shall" statements, as this action would violate the consensus process used to approve this standard.

This Technical Standard was prepared following requirements for due process, consensus, and approval as required by the U.S. Department of Energy Standards Program. Consensus is established when substantial agreement has been reached by all members of the writing team and the Technical Standard has been approved through the Department of Energy directives approval process (REVCOM). Substantial agreement means much more than a simple majority, but not necessarily unanimity. Consensus requires that all views and objections be considered, and that a concerted effort be made toward their resolution.

1.   SCOPE. This document provides Department of Energy (DOE) field offices and associated facilities/sites with a standard methodology for adapting the Department's tactical doctrine to site-specific needs in a coherent, consistent, and repeatable fashion. This Technical Standard, while based on time-tested military doctrine and tactics, is not intended to describe all acceptable methods for meeting the requirements of DOE Order (O) 470.3B, *Graded Security Protection (GSP) Policy*, or its successor; DOE O 470.4B, *Safeguards and Security Program*, or its successor; and DOE O 473.3, *Protection Program Operations*, or its successor, for the protection of nuclear weapons and components, special nuclear material (SNM), or targets subject to radiological or toxicological sabotage. However, it does describe a consistent and acceptable approach to defensive planning for both new and existing facilities/sites.

2.   PURPOSE. The purpose of this Technical Standard is to provide site/facility operators with an accepted compliance-based process to develop site specific protection strategies to meet protection program policy objectives for implementation of the tactical doctrine contained in DOE O 470.4B. This Technical Standard is not intended to require the use of any strategy, tactic, or technology. Examples which have been proven to be effective are presented to provide users options. All proposed plans ultimately should be examined for viability based upon cost benefit analyses.

3.   APPLICABILITY. This Technical Standard is intended primarily for use by management, operations, security, and vulnerability analysts at sites/facilities possessing nuclear weapons and components, Category I SNM, or targets subject to radiological/toxicological sabotage. Additionally, the processes and principles contained in this Technical Standard are suitable for employment at any other type of site/facility where planning for a defense against an attack may be appropriate, whether the mission is denial of access, denial of task, or containment. An assessment checklist that can be used to evaluate the adequacy of defensive plans is provided (Appendix D).

4.   REFERENCES. References commonly used in the Safeguards and Security Program are located in the Health, Safety, and Security Policy Information Resource located at http://pir.pnl.gov.

   a.   DOE O 470.3B, *Graded Security Protection (GSP) Policy*, dated 08-12-2008.

   b.   DOE O 470.4B, *Safeguards and Security Program*, dated 02-23-2011.

   c.   DOE O 473.3, *Protection Program Operations*, dated 06-27-2011.

   d.   DOE Standard for Vulnerability Assessments (DOE-STD-1192-2010).

   e.   *Leavenworth Papers No. 1: The Evolution of US Army Tactical Doctrine,*

1946-76, Doughty RA, Maj., Combat Studies Institute, Fort Leavenworth, Kansas, 1979.

f. *MCDP 1: Warfighting*, U.S. Marine Corps, 06-20-1997.

g. *MCDP 5: Planning*, U.S. Marine Corps, 07-21-1997.

h. *FM 3-0: Operations*, U.S. Army, 6-14-2001.

i. *FM 3-90: Tactics*, U.S. Army, 07-04-2001.

j. *FM 5-33: Terrain Analysis*, U.S. Army, 07-11-1990.

k. *FM 21-75: Combat Skills of the Soldier*, U.S. Army, 08-03-1984.

l. *Joint Publication 3-15: Barriers, Obstacles, and Mine Warfare for Joint Operations*, Joint Chiefs of Staff, 04-26-2007.

m. *MSTP Pamphlet 5-0.6: Relative Combat Power Assessment Users Guide*, U.S. Marine Corps, 10-2001.

n. *Principles of War*, von Clausewitz C, "On War," 1942.

o. *The Secret of Future Victories*, Gorman PF, General (Retired), U.S. Army, 02-1992.

5. ACRONYMS AND DEFINITIONS. Definitions and acronyms commonly used in the Safeguards and Security Program are located in the Health, Safety and Security Policy Information Resource located at http://pir.pnl.gov.

a. Acronyms.

   (1) DOE: U.S. Department of Energy

   (2) GSP: DOE's Graded Security Protection Policy

   (3) LOS: line of sight

   (4) MEL: maximum engagement line

   (5) PF: protective force

   (6) SNM: special nuclear material

   (7) SOF: sector of fire

   (8) SPO: security police officer

   (9) WMD: weapon of mass destruction

b. <u>Definitions</u>.

    (1)   <u>Denial of Access Missions</u> require the implementation of a protection strategy designed to engage and neutralize an adversary before he has gained access to the material or asset.

    (2)   <u>Denial of Task Missions</u> require the implementation of a protection strategy designed to prevent and/or to neutralize a threat so as to preclude the completion of specific tasks.

    (3)   <u>Containment Missions</u> require the implementation of a protection strategy designed to prevent an adversary or SNM from leaving a particular space, structure, or facility.

    (4)   <u>Lines of Communication(s)</u> are routes that connect an operating unit with its base of support.

    (5)   <u>Barriers</u> are coordinated series of natural or fabricated impediments that direct, restrict, limit, delay, or deny entry into a designated area.

    (6)   <u>Obstacles</u> are any obstruction designed or employed to disrupt, fix, turn, or block the movement of an opposing force. As with barriers, obstacles can exist naturally, be manmade, or may be a combination of the two.

    (7)   <u>Observation</u> is the ability to see over a particular area to acquire targets. While visibility is weather dependent and may be variable, observation is terrain dependent and is relatively consistent. Generally, the best observation is obtained from the highest terrain in an area.

    (8)   <u>Fields of Fire</u> are areas or sectors that can be covered effectively by direct and/or indirect weapons fire from a given point.

    (9)   <u>Cover</u> is the protection from the effects of direct, indirect, or air-to-ground weapons fire.

    (10)   <u>Concealment</u> provides protection from observation from the air, the ground, or both.

    (11)   <u>Intervisibility</u> is the ability to see from one object or position to another.

    (12)   <u>Economy of Force</u> is the principle of employing all available combat power in the most effective way possible, in an attempt to allocate a minimum of essential combat power to any secondary efforts. It is the judicious employment and distribution of forces toward the primary objective of any conflict.

6.   DEFENSIVE PLANNING.

    a.   Concept.

        (1)   Any adversarial incursion against a DOE target is expected to be brief and violent, so preparedness is paramount. Site terrain throughout the DOE complex varies from urban landscapes through forested mountain slopes to sparsely settled deserts and plains. Even though DOE specifies the size and capabilities of the adversary group against which a site is expected to be successful, each potential target for unauthorized access or actions presents a unique planning and resource challenge. Further, DOE protective forces (PFs) perform many routine duties such as access control, checks of doors and gates, alarm system monitoring, traffic control, etc. Therefore, a hybrid deployment model that combines fixed and mobile positions has been determined to provide the best capability to meet all protection program needs across the spectrum of both routine and emergency duties. Throughout the planning process, due consideration should be given to the adversary threat analysis and capabilities as described in DOE O 470.3B.

        (2)   As stated in the tactical doctrine outlined in DOE O 470.4B, generally at DOE sites/facilities possessing nuclear weapons and components, Category I SNM, or targets subject to radiological/toxicological sabotage, defensive plans may involve an area defense with fixed strong points, or fighting positions, that encompass a target. Those positions lie within a concentric arrangement of intrusion detection systems and barriers designed to detect, assess, delay, engage, and neutralize the adversary as far from the target as possible. Early detection and assessment, especially if significant delaying mechanisms are in place, can provide a substantial advantage to defending forces by enabling response times that ensure proper preparation. One example of a system capable of providing early detection is the Stabilized Panoramic Intrusion Detection and Recognition System (Figure 1), although sites have also had success with radar systems and unattended ground sensors. As detection and assessment degrade, delaying capabilities should be enhanced, response times reduced, or both. This will permit adequate preparedness of the PF and timely engagement of the adversarial force.

Figure 1. Stabilized Panoramic Intrusion Detection and Recognition System

(3)   The overall aim of the tactical doctrine is to ensure engagement of an adversary force as early as practical; to inflict casualties on the adversary force before it encounters the main line of resistance; and to compel the adversarial force to advance from that point against a well-prepared, heavily armed, well-protected defense. This will reduce PF casualties and provide a defense as unaffected by adversary numbers and tactics as possible. Figure 2 below shows the number of required security police officers (SPOs) required to defeat an adversary attack as a function of number of attackers.

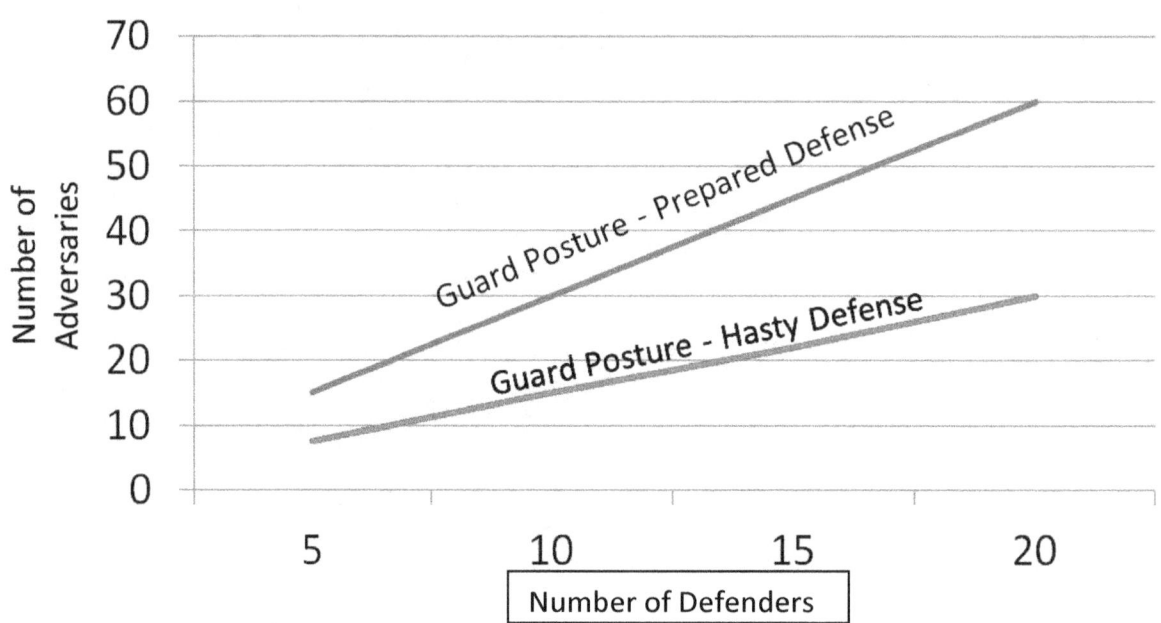

Figure 2. Effect of Preparation on Defensive Effectiveness[1]

(4)   PF personnel are assumed to be in one of two postures: 1) deployed to partially protected locations just before an adversary enters planned fields

---

[1] This Figure is consistent with broad planning factors found in *Relative Combat Power Assessment Users Guide.* It is provided only to illustrate the relative differences in preferred versus hasty defenses.

of fire (hasty defense); or 2) occupying well-designed defensive positions when the adversary enters planned fields of fire (prepared defense). Clearly, the number of PF personnel required to defeat a given number of adversaries is optimized when the PF is placed in advantageous defensive positions.

(5)   A well-designed defensive plan will reduce adversary tactical choices by:

    (a)   The use of barriers to eliminate approach routes;

    (b)   Early and precise detection, for example, pinpointing sniper fire with an acoustic detection system (Figure 3), to allow early engagement; and

    (c)   The use of mobile forces to evaluate potential threats and "channel" adversary forces into prepared killing zones.

Figure 3. Sniper Detection System

(6)   The plan will also encourage the PF to fight smart by:

    (a)   Forcing the adversary to face prepared positions;

    (b)   Using tactical teams to improve effectiveness against larger adversary formations;

    (c)   Taking advantage of terrain and natural obstacles; and

    (d)   Minimizing reliance on complex or aggressive schemes of maneuver.

b.   Defensive Planning Principles.

(1)   Prepare the Defensive Area. The proper analysis, design, and construction of the physical layout of the defensive area are essential to ensure the most effective employment of all available resources (e.g., weapons, obscurants, video surveillance, etc.) to neutralize an adversary and to

sustain minimal friendly casualties and damage to the site. Sound barrier and fire planning that take full advantage of the local terrain are fundamental to that effort; therefore, such planning should be based on a thorough analysis of all terrain features surrounding the target. (See Appendix A.)

(a)   Barrier Planning. A strong barrier plan is central to an effective defensive strategy. At the operational level, the primary use of barriers is to restrict an adversary's maneuvering options or to permit friendly maneuver options. Operational barriers and obstacles may be created by the composite effect of many closely coordinated tactical obstacles or by the reinforcement of natural obstacles to form large terrain or massive obstacles (Figure 4). Employment at the tactical level is normally done to achieve offensive or defensive objectives, to include enhancement of friendly direct/indirect fires, to delay/destroy adversary formations, or to enable economy of force. The number of points and avenues of approach to a target should be minimized to assist in creating a favorable force ratio for defensive responders. To ensure the maximum effectiveness of each member of the PF and all available weaponry, an adversary attack force should be channeled into attrition areas covered by interlocking bands of fire from hardened fighting positions that provide protection to the defenders. (See Appendix B.)

Figure 4. Rip Rap Outside the Perimeter Intrusion Detection and Assessment System to Impair Adversary Movement

1   Major natural terrain features and a focus on potential adversary avenues of approach and tactics provide the foundation for the development of an obstacle or barrier plan. The PF should be able to exploit the benefits of

7

occupying the terrain where the fight may occur, engaging the adversary from positions that provide a clear advantage. A terrain analysis should be conducted as a joint effort involving vulnerability analysts, security planners, and PF supervisors. Starting at each specific target location, all aspects of the surrounding terrain should be examined in a 360 degree arc extending beyond the site's perimeter. The analysis should be initiated with a close examination of the facility's/site's as-built drawings, topographic maps, and diagrams and then be followed by walking over as much of the area to be protected as possible. Attention should be paid to likely avenues of approach (such as depressions, culverts, streams, hills, vegetation, roads), buildings, obstacles (both natural and manmade), and any other site improvement or feature that could afford advantage or disadvantage to either friendly or adversary forces.

<u>2</u> The terrain analysis should dictate the location and types of barriers, mutually supporting hardened fighting positions, direct and indirect fire weapons systems, and observation points. It should identify fields of fire and dead spaces and consider the potential impact of weather (e.g., decreased visibility due to snow, rain, dust/sand storms or fog) or other natural phenomena.

<u>3</u> DOE O 473.3 contains requirements for the construction of specific types and locations of security areas and barriers to protect sensitive national assets. The barrier plan should provide for adequate shielding and standoff from vehicle-borne improvised explosive devices and for limiting the ability of airborne improvised explosive devices to impact key defensive positions and primary target buildings.

(b) <u>Fire Planning.</u>

<u>1</u> Defensive fire plans should ensure that high volumes of increasingly intensive fire can be brought to bear on an attacking adversary from its earliest detection through its final approach to a target. The battlefield should be cleared of all non-essential structures and vegetation. Primary and alternate mutually supporting fighting positions should be established to ensure that interlocking bands of fire can be delivered into kill zones into which the adversary has been forced through effective barrier design and placement and PF maneuver elements.

2   Crew-served weapons are most effective when deployed in fixed, hardened posts with good observation over the battlefield (Figure 5). At sites where armored vehicles are employed, consideration should be given to the construction of revetments from which the primary weapons systems of the vehicles can deliver effective fire. Defensive fire plans should be illustrated using diagrams or overlays of the area surrounding the target to ensure that all obstacles, barriers, and avenues of approach are addressed adequately and that no uncovered access to the target remains. Range cards that identify specific points on the battlefield upon which fire can be delivered, along with distances to those points, should be developed and placed at each fixed fighting position. (See Appendix C.)

NOTE: To be effective, all barriers/obstacles should be covered by means of detection and assessment and, where possible, observation and/or fire from one or more defensive positions. Barriers/obstacles without coverage by a means of detection and assessment are of little value unless they are insurmountable to adversary penetration. In all cases, detection, assessment, and coverage by fire greatly increase a barrier's/obstacle's defensive value.

Figure 5. Crew-Served Weapon System. The Bearcat Mounted Dillon M134 D Mini Gun, stationed in the protected area perimeter, allows a PF to engage hostile threats with an overwhelming rate of fire.

(2)   <u>Integrate All Aspects of the Defensive Plan.</u> Integrate all elements of the defensive plan to maximize effectiveness and efficiency. This is accomplished by publishing the plan as a single document to make sure that no critical questions or issues are left unanswered. In any case, each aspect should be cross-referenced to ensure adequate coordination is

accomplished. For example, multiple layers of detection and delay should be employed and coupled with appropriate technologies to enhance PF capabilities. The defensive fire plan should overlay the barrier plan so that effective fire can be delivered on the adversary while it is negotiating obstacles or using a prepared revetment for cover. The tactical doctrine contained in DOE O 470.4B contains a list of considerations that is not exhaustive but may be useful to a defensive planner. (See paragraph 6.c, Tactical Considerations, below.)

(3) Make the Adversary Fight to the Target. The "gold standard" for any defensive plan is to neutralize an attacking force before it can reach the target; therefore, it is essential that an incursion be detected, assessed, and engaged as far from the target as possible. Plans should include a means to assess remote alarms, either by means of technology or deployment of PF tactical teams. If the plan calls for assessment and early, close engagement by PF personnel then the staged withdrawal of those forces, under covering fire, to prepared defensive positions should be addressed. Aspects of the defensive plan that are essential to the success of the PF include:

(a) Multiple layers of detection, beginning as far from the target as terrain and technology allow;

(b) One or more viable means of assessing adversary capabilities that may include closed circuit television, radar, sonic systems, and/or active patrolling by exterior forces (Figure 6);

(c) Effective denial of adversary approach routes that are unfavorable to the defense;

(d) Multiple layers of delay along remaining adversary approach routes, each covered by effective weapons fire;

(e) Carefully planned interlocking fields of fire from mutually supporting positions; and

(f) Integration of planned mobile unit movements with defensive fire plans and barrier plans.

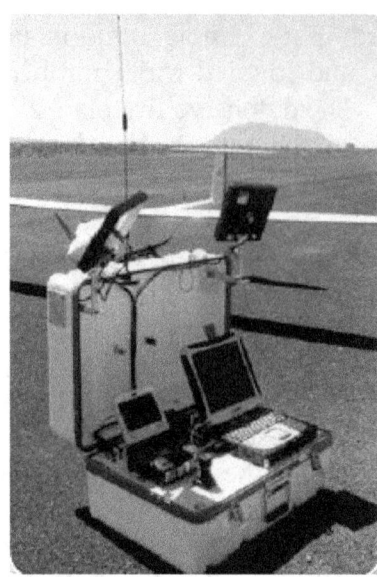

Figure 6. Unmanned Aerial Vehicle Detection Assessment

(4)   <u>Make the Target Location Deadly.</u> In addition to the pre-positioning of PF personnel in protected posts at or near the target, consideration may be given to the installation of active or passive denial systems. DOE O 473.3 addresses the use of activated barriers, deterrents, and obscurants (Figure 7) as denial of access/denial of task systems that may be integrated into the target defensive planning process.

Figure 7. CO$_2$ Active Denial System

(5)   <u>Manage the Site Population.</u> An attack could occur while the site is engaged in a fully operational mode; therefore, an effective defensive plan should accommodate the presence of a large number of workers, both within and outside of the target area. Plans should consider the survival of operations workers and the potential for their interference with the defense by obstructing lines of observation, maneuver, or fire. In addition to routinely limiting the number of personnel and vehicles permitted in the target area, procedures should be developed to ensure that employees are trained on their responsibilities and actions in the event of an attack. Realistically, few operations workers can be expected to give much thought to the eventuality of an attack on the site; therefore, to supplement

11

the plans, the workers should be reminded periodically of the potential for an adversarial incursion and the expectations for their actions.

c. <u>Tactical Considerations.</u> A sound defensive plan should address the overall site-specific PF tactical employment necessary to counter adversarial threats, to include the organization and disposition of routine posts and patrols, plans for the constitution/reconstitution of tactical teams, armament, vehicles, and equipment. Tactics, techniques, and procedures for re-entry, recapture, fresh pursuit, and recovery operations should be included. Placement of posts and patrols is dependent on vulnerability and terrain analyses along with the resultant barrier and fire plans.

(1) To ensure that the maximum number of on-shift armed PF personnel are available to counter an assault at any time, unarmed officers should perform routine duties not related directly to protection of the target (e.g., acting as administrative escorts or manning noncritical access control posts that may not be suitable for automation, etc.).

(2) The PF disposition should consist primarily of personnel in well prepared positions augmented by a relatively small number of specially trained officers, to include Special Response Teams (SRT) who could maneuver against the adversary if required. Careful consideration should be given to the assignment of the most highly trained, qualified, and physically capable personnel to posts/patrols/duties that are most likely to require extended maneuvering on foot and/or an advanced skill set. Officers trained to less stringent requirements can be employed effectively in fixed posts or operating armored vehicles with the expectation of engaging the adversary using the vehicle's on-board weapon systems. The employment of remotely operated weapon systems might be completely reserved to those SPOs (Figure 8).

Figure 8. Remotely Operated Weapons System

(3) Effective command and control, as well as the survival of PF members in a fluid combat situation, are greatly enhanced by the PF responding in

12

tactical teams consisting of no fewer than two officers. Should it be necessary for a site to employ single-person patrols or posts, specific rally points should be selected so that tactical teams can be constituted prior to engaging the adversary. One leader should be designated for each team.

(4)   Mutually supporting, stationary hardened-fighting positions placed in close proximity to the target should be manned by officers armed with crew-served automatic weapons. Such posts can be occupied at all times by one or more members of a team or serve as a response post in event of an attack. In the event the posts are not occupied at all times, provisions should be made to detect and/or to deny adversary access when unoccupied.

(5)   Armored vehicle crews should consist of at least two officers, one of whom is designated as the vehicle commander. Depending on the tactical situation, armored vehicles may respond as maneuver elements to engage the adversary force directly or to position themselves in prepared positions, preferably revetments designed to cover barriers, chokepoints, or kill zones.

(6)   Vertical insertions by an adversary using parachutes, helicopters, fast ropes, ultra light aircraft, etc., should be considered when planning tactical responses to various threats. When possible, insertion and/or movement from the insertion point should be made more difficult by barriers/obstacles and/or by defensive fires. If likely insertion points cannot be covered adequately by fixed fighting positions surrounding the target, then responding SPOs should move to preplanned positions that have good observation of those insertion points along with clear fields of fire. If an adversary force succeeds in landing, rapid containment of the landing zone is essential to neutralize the threat before the attackers organize and move out. The PF commander should be prepared to rapidly commit available units to secure an advantage over the adversary while it remains concentrated in the insertion area.

(7)   If a site's defensive strategy is based on containment of the adversary at the target rather than denial of access or of task, and if the attackers have penetrated to the target, then the tactical response should require the PF to assume prepared positions with good observation of the target area and clear, interlocking fields of fire. Since, in this instance, it is unlikely that PF personnel would routinely occupy defensive positions around the target, plans should accommodate the time required for the defending force to move from its primary posts and/or patrols once detection of the adversary has occurred.

d.   Command, Control, Communications, and Intelligence. Central to effective command, control, communications, and intelligence is a secure command center possessing both primary and alternate means of communication with fixed and maneuver elements of the PF. The defensive plan should address those specific issues, and it should address any other means of communications that may be employed effectively at a given site (e.g., signal flares, public address systems, etc.). A system for identifying friendly forces should be adopted so that effective controls can be exercised over fire discipline and maneuver elements to minimize casualties from friendly fire. A well defined command structure from the on-site commander down to the individual tactical team leaders is essential. Depending on the size of the facility/site and the number of targets, consideration should be given to the establishment of sectors within the overall command structure. Sector commanders would then be responsible for controlling the tactical teams and vehicles assigned to that sector. Finally, there should be provision made for dissemination of tactical intelligence during the engagement to designated members of the command and control team and to other defenders.

e.   Logistics.   Where practicable, provisions should be made in the plan for the prepositioning of post-specific weapons, equipment, and ammunition as well as emergency items such as fire suppression devices and first-aid kits. Consideration should be given to how ammunition would be resupplied during a protracted firefight and to a means of treating and evacuating wounded officers to medical facilities.

f.   Re-Entry/Recapture Operations.   Availability of a re-entry/recapture reserve, SRT personnel, should be maintained throughout a battle. This ensures the ability to re-enter/ recapture the target in the event that an adversary reaches the target area. This reserve, usually an SRT, should be considered as a reserve element beyond the element tasked with preventing adversary access to target facilities. While the re-entry/recapture element can be used at the discretion of the tactical commander to decisively influence the battle, it should be remembered that if that element is committed to the fight too early, there may not be sufficient strength remaining to mount a re-entry/recapture operation. The defensive plan should contain target-specific tactics, techniques, procedures, and equipment needed to perform the re-entry/recapture mission. The potential for the involvement of hostages should be addressed. Note that if SNM is at risk, regaining control of the material is the primary consideration; as affirmed in the tactical doctrine outlined in DOE O 470.4B, the security of nuclear assets shall hold priority over personnel.

g.   Pursuit and Recovery Operations.   If an adversary is able to leave the site with an asset, it is likely that the PF has suffered heavy losses. In that case, pursuit and recovery operations should, out of necessity, be conducted by whatever elements remain. Therefore, it is essential that all armed PF personnel be trained to support pursuit and recovery operations and that the defensive plan address that eventuality. With the notable exception of nuclear/special weapons security, there is no comparable military tactical equivalent that has as its objective the recovery of a specific asset. Local and federal law enforcement agencies could play a vital role; therefore, it is extremely important to maintain current memoranda of agreement/memoranda of understanding with local and Federal law enforcement agencies that address specific roles as well as how pursuit and recovery plans can be exercised. The fresh pursuit guidelines contained in the DOE O 473.3 (Appendix A, Annex 1) apply and should be consulted when developing this portion of the defensive plan.

h.   Weapons of Mass Destruction (WMD). An effective defensive plan should include site-specific tactics, techniques, and procedures for operating in a WMD environment. The plan should emphasize how a WMD attack may impact tactical responses, especially how timelines will be affected by the need to don appropriate protective equipment as well as how that equipment will influence individual capabilities. A WMD attack would create its own special set of anxieties for personnel, so WMD response planning, training, and exercising is extremely important.

7.   MANAGEMENT CONSIDERATIONS.

a.   Format. It is a given that PF management at all sites have in place site-specific orders and procedures, to include site security plans that address the defense of targets. Therefore, rather than setting forth a format for a defensive plan, this Technical Standard provides the means to ensure that existing planning documentation includes the points that are essential to the effective preservation of vital national security assets.

b.   Training.

(1)   An element at least as important as the tactical doctrine and sound defensive planning is the level of PF training required for success. It is absolutely essential that the PF be trained for the fight and that each person should:

(a)   Individually understand the response plan and his or her part in it;

(b)   Be proficient in tactical movement and tactical teaming;

(c)   Thoroughly understand his or her legal authorities; and

(d)   Be proficient with all assigned weapons and equipment.

(2)   Training should be in the most realistic environment possible to support the "train as you fight" concept. The use of engagement simulation systems such as laser enhanced training weapons or other systems that require acquisition of, and firing at, a human target is a very effective training method. If such training can be conducted from time to time in the locations to be defended, it should provide a great advantage to the SPOs in an actual engagement. When it is not feasible to conduct engagement simulations or equivalent training activities in actual locations, PF members who may respond to particular locations would benefit from sufficient access to those areas to gain familiarity with physical features, target locations, and other information that would assist

them in their response activities. Even if the actual protected locations are often unavailable for training, great progress can be made in teaching tactical maneuvers, team tactics, and basic combat skills during limited response exercises employing engagement-simulation-system-equipped weapons, when the location is available for training.

c.   <u>Implementation.</u> A sound defensive plan should employ a combination of highly mobile teams using fire and maneuver in addition to natural and designed obstacles/barriers to channel adversaries into attrition areas covered by interlocking fields of fire from fixed, hardened fighting positions. The mobile teams may be mounted in light armored vehicles equipped with automatic weapons in the outer layers of the defense, but often maneuver on foot nearer to the target areas. The role of mobile teams is to influence the adversary assault team so that they encounter the stationary positions and become fixed in place or are forced to advance against overwhelming weapons fire. The mobile teams may also provide a final neutralization of the adversary assault team when their progress toward the target is halted. While this defensive scheme depends on the PF to provide much of the neutralization of the adversary, the SPOs may not be able to perform this task with efficiency unless all aspects of the defensive plan are fully integrated into the site's tactical concept. (See Appendix C for information on SPOs and defensive fire planning.) Appendix D contains a checklist designed to assist in the completion of the steps necessary for the development of an effective site defensive plan.

1. GENERAL. In the context of Department of Energy protection program planning, terrain analysis is the process of interpreting natural and manmade features of a geographic area to determine their effects on site defensive operations. Major natural terrain features and a focus on the adversary provide the foundation for the development of an obstacle or barrier plan and a subsequent defensive fire plan. To ensure that the proper results are obtained, adequate analytical tools and data should be assembled during preparation for the task. These may include: topographical maps (Figure 9); survey reports; diagrams of the site that depict as much detail as possible; photographs, to include aerial photographs and satellite imagery; hydrological surveys; climate and weather information; and any other data that may be useful.

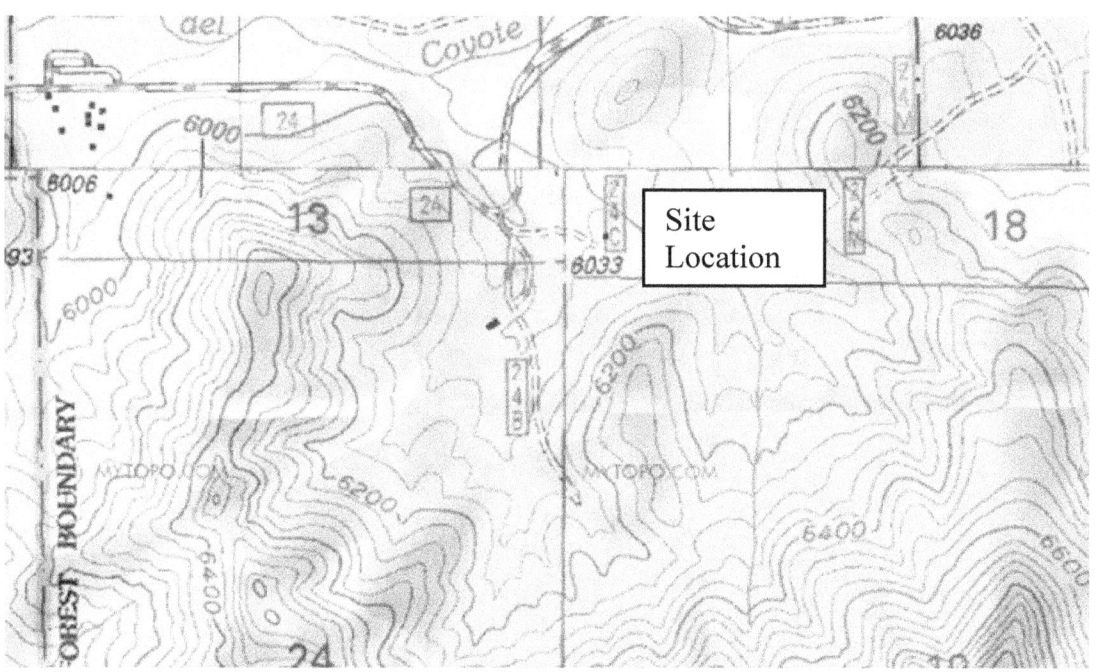

Figure 9. Topography and Terrain Consideration

2. PROCESS. To be effective, the terrain analysis should be the product of a methodical, detail-oriented approach. Even though the collection, review, analysis, and consolidation of the documents and imagery may appear to be laborious and time consuming, this process likely will enhance the efficiency of the process dramatically.

    a. A terrain analysis team should be selected that consists of representatives of as many disciplines as possible, including vulnerability analysts, security planners, protective force supervisors, safety representatives, engineers, communication specialists, and site operations management. Each discipline should approach the analysis from a different perspective, which will prove to be valuable as the defensive planning process progresses.

b.	Team members should have a solid understanding of their objectives and, particularly, how their report may be used as the basis for the development or refinement of the site defensive plan.

c.	To determine the effect of terrain on the general courses of action available to both protective force and adversary forces, analysts should evaluate it in terms of its defensive applications: observation and fields of fire, cover and concealment, obstacles, key terrain, and avenues of approach.

(1)	Observation Locations and Fields of Fire. The evaluation of observation locations and fields of fire identifies potential engagement areas, defensible terrain, weapons system positions, and where maneuvering forces are most vulnerable to observation and fires.

(2)	Cover and Concealment.

(a)	Cover can sometimes be used to protect a force from observation, in which case, the object providing cover is also providing concealment. However, cover and concealment do not always equate. Some examples are vegetation, cultural features, geographical relief features, drainage areas, weather conditions, and darkness which provide concealment, whereas rocks, buildings, and large berms provide cover from weapons fire and shrapnel.

(b)	If an attacking force can move forward under concealment, its chances of achieving surprise increases. Concealed and covered approach routes are important to an adversary; therefore, they should be minimized.

(3)	Obstacles. Obstacles may be any natural or manmade terrain feature that stops, impedes, slows, or diverts movement.

(4)	Key (or Decisive) Terrain. Key terrain is any terrain feature (natural or manmade) that, if controlled, gives a marked advantage to whoever controls it. Key or decisive terrain should be controlled by occupation, by fires, or by maneuvering tactical teams.

(5)	Avenues of Approach. An avenue of approach is an air or ground route of an attacking force leading to its objective or to key terrain in its path.

d.	Characteristics of potential impacts to communication systems available to the adversary and/or to the protective force (bridges, tunnels, sharp curves, steep grades, etc.), hydrology (river/stream depth, width, velocity, bottom material, bank height, and ford sites), drainage (gulleys, swales, culverts, and arroyos), buildings, and potential landing or drop zones should be identified and evaluated.

e.   The potential effects of climate and weather on adversary movement cannot be ignored or underestimated. For example, rain may render an otherwise navigable terrain feature, such as an arroyo, impassable; therefore, the likelihood of an approach through that terrain could be reduced in adverse weather conditions. Also, care should be exercised in the placement of, or dependence on, defensive positions that could be rendered untenable under certain weather conditions.

f.   To ensure that defensive fighting positions can be mutually supportable or that an area between a fighting position and the security area perimeter is clear, line-of-sight (LOS) determinations should be made. To complete an LOS determination, verify that one location can be seen from another under all seasonal conditions and that a terrain feature is not blocking the view. LOS determinations can identify defiladed areas for mobile teams and/or places where the effects of direct fire on attacking forces may be masked. The best way to determine intervisibility is to physically occupy each location and note the position and nature of all features that interfere with LOS. When that is not possible or before the initial terrain evaluation is completed, topographical maps and aerial photographs can be very helpful. This information plays an important role in the development of the site defensive plan. If LOS obstructions cannot be removed, then some type of compensatory measures should be adopted to cover all dead spaces.

g.   The team should prepare a report that consists of diagrams and sketches of the site illustrating prominent terrain features, structures, and dead space with existing obstacles and barriers depicted on overlays (Figure 10). Narrative explanations of each illustration should be included. The format and content of the report should also be site-specific and dependent on preference, site/facility location, size, targets, geography, configuration, etc., and whether a terrain analysis report has been prepared previously.

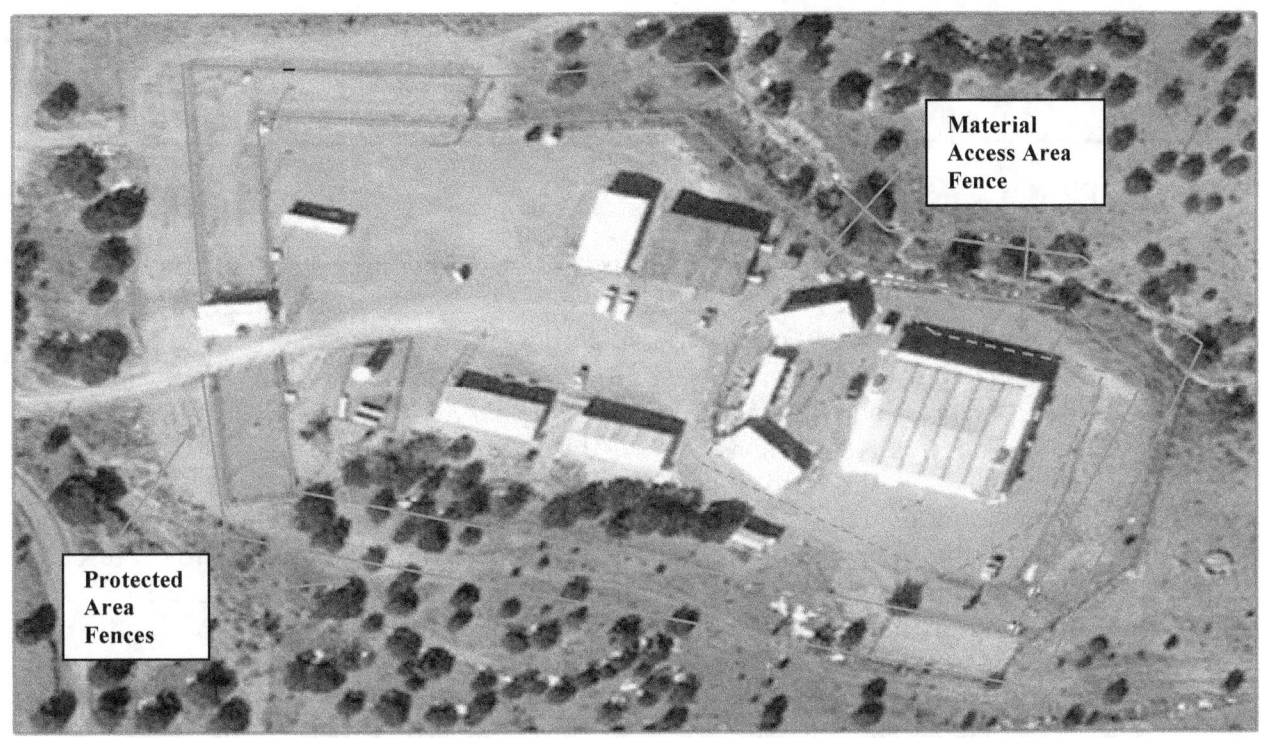

Figure 10. Layout with Perimeter Fences and Protected Area Fences Added

3.   SUMMARY. A detailed analysis of the site's terrain is essential since all elements of the defensive plan rely on it for the development of vulnerability analyses, determinations of likely avenues of approach, the locations of hardened fighting positions, placement of crew-served weapons, barrier plans, defensive fire plans, and preplanned tactical responses for maneuver elements.

APPENDIX B. BARRIER PLANNING

1. <u>GENERAL.</u>

    a.   The design and placement of barriers is dictated by the threat and the terrain analysis as well as by site operational considerations. Therefore, it is essential that as many disciplines as possible participate in the barrier planning process, to include vulnerability analysts, security planners, protective force (PF) supervisors, safety representatives, engineers, and site operations management. The team may consist of the same persons who conducted the terrain analysis.

    b.   The barrier planning process helps determine the types of barriers to be employed and how best to position them to meet a variety of objectives, e.g., to decrease blast overpressure effects at certain locations, increase the effectiveness of friendly fire and maneuver, and to deny or channel the movement of an adversary. Properly integrated obstacles, obscurants, and fires help to take the initiative from the adversary and deny its objectives. While an adversary may use a barrier as cover and/or concealment, the barrier may still provide value to the defense by impeding the rapid advance of the opposing force and allowing time for the defending force to adjust and maneuver to the attack axis. The selection of a particular type or design of barrier for a specific application or threat is limited only by the imagination and resources of the planners and compliance with existing policy. This appendix is not intended to present a compendium of available commercial products; nor would it be practical to offer recommendations for every situation that may be encountered on any given site.

    c.   The effectiveness of obstacles and barriers is enhanced considerably when they are covered by observation and fire.

    d.   The use of revetments to provide shelter or protection against vehicle borne bomb attacks is an effective countermeasure when applied to fixed sites for the protection of fixed fighting positions. A protective wall, consisting of soil, sandbags, a metal wall, or concrete barrier, etc. for gun emplacements and other equipment or personnel, can protect the position from bomb fragmentation and weapons fire.

2. <u>PROCESS.</u>

    a.   The team should be selected and thoroughly briefed on the objectives to be accomplished (i.e., to ensure that each target is provided with the strongest defense possible by augmenting existing terrain features with additional barriers designed to detect/impede an adversarial incursion and to channel attackers into preplanned kill zones of interlocking weapons fire).

b.	The detailed terrain analysis and all supporting documentation should be provided to the team for review as the basis for the barrier plan.

c.	DOE O 473.3 should be consulted to ensure compliance with barrier requirements for specific types of security areas. As long as minimum policy requirements are met, the selection of particular types of barriers for specific applications is a site management decision.

d.	If team members are familiar with the site and its existing facilities and structures, initial conceptual design and layout can usually be accomplished in a table-top forum using the topographical maps and site sketches from the terrain analysis.

e.	To ensure uniform perspectives by all team members, the terrain walk to verify the barrier design and placement resulting from the table-top sessions should be performed by the entire team.

f.	Remote electronic detection and assessment devices should be integrated into the barrier plan along with remotely operated weapon systems where practicable. These systems can be used to enhance PF capabilities by providing a means to detect an adversary incursion as early as possible, thereby, enabling rapid responses to assess and to neutralize attackers as far from the target as possible.

g.	Diagrams/sketches of the site should illustrate prominent terrain features, structures, and dead space with obstacles and barriers depicted on overlays that can be modified if necessary.

h.	To ensure the effectiveness of the barrier plan, initial validation should be conducted using table-top exercises consisting of likely attack scenarios.

i.	As barriers are constructed / emplaced, consideration should be given to a continuing validation process of limited scope performance testing. After the defensive fire plan is completed, the barriers should be validated with full-scale force-on-force performance testing.

3.	SUMMARY.

a.	The primary reasons for installing a system of obstacles and barriers (Figure 11 and Figure 12) on and outside the defensive perimeter are:

(1)	To aid in the early detection, delay, and disruption of adversary activity;

(2)	To introduce a vulnerability to enemy maneuvering that can be exploited by the site PF;

(3)	To cause the adversary to divide into smaller attacking forces;

(4)	To interfere with the adversary's command and control;

(5)   To exploit the capabilities of PF weapon systems by delaying attacking forces in an engagement area or kill zone;

(6)   To provide protection for site targets and personnel from vehicle-borne or airborne improvised explosive devices; and

(7)   To protect PF personnel from adversary maneuvering and infiltration.

Figure 11. Secure Gate

Figure 12. Vehicle Barriers

b.   The barrier plan built upon a detailed terrain analysis constitutes a vitally important and basic part of the development of the defensive fire plan. To be most effective, all obstacles/barriers should be covered by either direct observation or electronically and, when possible, by fire (Figure 13). Obstacles and barriers should be designed and constructed to enhance the ability of PF tactical teams and/or armored vehicles to maneuver effectively to force attackers into kill zones of interlocking fire from fixed positions.

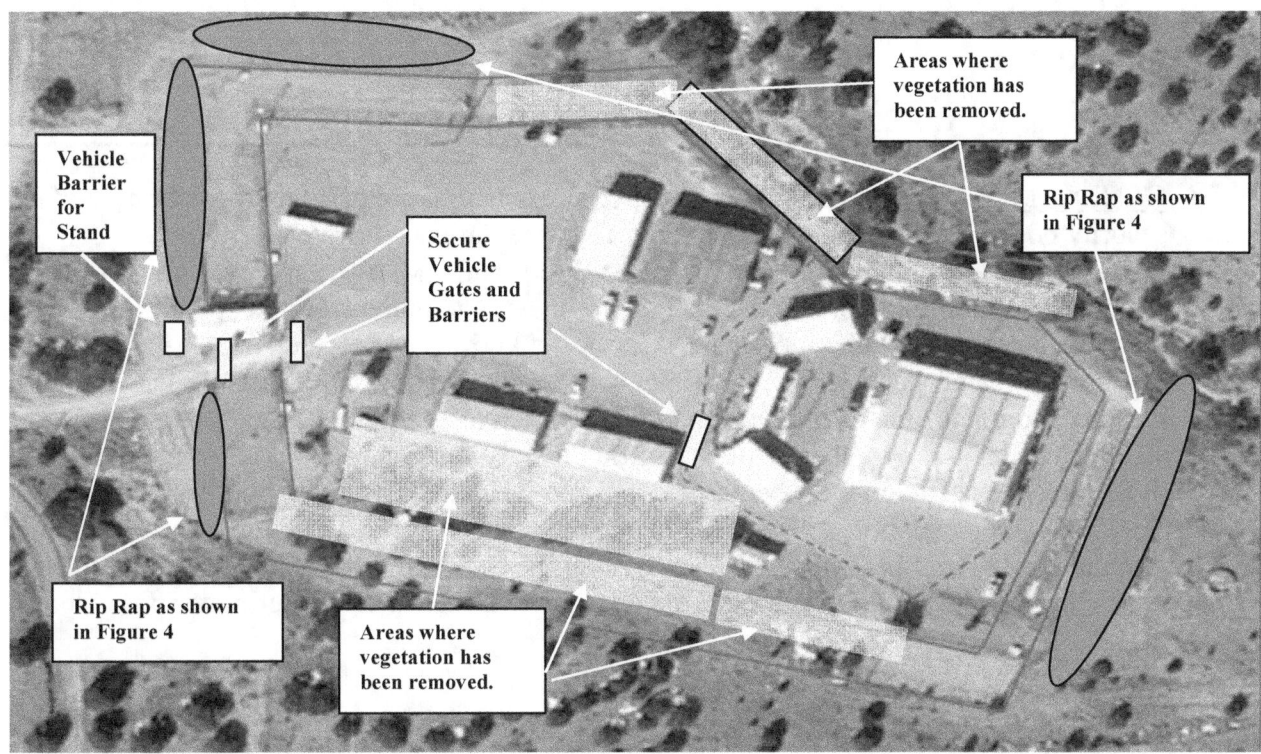

Figure 13. Layout with Vehicle Barriers, Rip Rap, and Secure Vehicle Gates Added. Vegetation has been removed from within the protected area.

APPENDIX C. DEFENSIVE FIRE PLANNING

1.   <u>GENERAL.</u> The success of a site's defense depends in large part on its positioning of security police officers and weapons; therefore, the defensive fire plan should be developed by a team consisting of those who are familiar with the site protective force structure, weapons, equipment, tactical deployment, and maneuvering capabilities. To position the weapons effectively, planners should know the characteristics, capabilities, and limitations of the weapons; the effects of terrain, and adversary capabilities. Each weapon should be able to engage the attacker effectively, and it is essential that the weapons can mass coordinated direct fire on the attacker. In addition to being capable of delivering direct fire on the adversary, every fixed and supplementary defensive position should be able to support adjacent defensive positions. If mutually supporting fire is not preplanned there is a very high probability that the attacker may be able to isolate and neutralize an unsupported fighting position making a breach of the perimeter possible.

2.   <u>PROCESS.</u>

    a.   Barrier planning should be completed prior to the development of defensive fire plans. Only then can hardened fighting positions be placed to take full advantage of natural and constructed obstacles. In order to be most effective, all barriers/obstacles should be covered by observation and/or fire from one or more defensive positions; otherwise, except for perhaps providing limited delay, barriers may provide little protection for the target and opportunities to engage the attacker with effective fire may be reduced.

    b.   The site diagram that depicts the barrier plan should be used as the basis for the development of the defensive fire plan to ensure that all obstacles, dead space, and likely avenues of approach are covered by observation and fire and that all fighting positions are mutually supporting. Hardened fighting positions should provide protection against anticipated adversary weapons but should also provide protection against the most commonly available PF weapons, enabling personnel in adjacent locations to clear close-in adversary threats by fire. Preliminary planning and initial fire plan sketches can be completed prior to a confirmatory terrain walk.

    c.   All fighting positions, whether fixed and hardened or supplemental, and armored vehicle response revetments should be assigned specific primary sectors of fire (SOFs) that overlap the SOF of adjacent positions on both sides completely around the entire defensive perimeter.

    d.   Range cards should be produced for each weapon system (other than handguns) assigned to, or likely to be deployed from, every fighting position; they function essentially as a subset of the overall defensive fire plan. A range card is a sketch of the assigned sector for which a tactical team with direct and/or indirect fire weapons is responsible. It aids in planning and controlling fields of fire and facilitates acquisition of targets during limited visibility. Each tactical team that is responsible for manning a response position should review the range card when assuming duty, noting any changes in the situation or terrain, and reporting those changes to their supervisor. This process ensures current information on the card. To prepare a range card, the following minimum information should be determined and depicted:

(1)   Sector of Fire (SOF). An SOF is a piece of the battlefield for which a tactical team or fighting position is responsible. Both primary and secondary sectors may be assigned to ensure fires are distributed around the perimeter.

    (a)   An SOF is assigned to cover possible adversary avenues of approach and should overlap adjacent sectors to provide the best use of suppressive fire and to cover areas that cannot be engaged effectively by a single weapon system.

    (b)   Left and right sector limits are assigned using prominent terrain features or easily recognizable objects such as large rocks, utility poles, fences, or stakes.

(2)   Target Reference Points. Target reference points are natural or manmade features within the SOF that can be used for target acquisition; range determination; and initiation, distribution, and controlling of fires. They should be depicted and numbered on the range card as well as on the defensive fire plan overlay in the command center.

(3)   Patrol Reference Points. Patrol reference points are natural or manmade features within an SOF that can be used for patrol or maneuver element checkpoints to enable the close coordination of supporting or suppressive fires with tactical team movement. They should be depicted and numbered on the range card as well as on the defensive fire plan overlay in the command center.

(4)   Dead Space. Dead space is any area that cannot be observed or covered by direct-fire systems within an SOF. All dead space within the sector should be identified to allow the planning of indirect fires (e.g., from grenade launchers) to cover that area. All security police officers and supervisors who may be responsible for delivering indirect fire into a dead space should walk the engagement area to ensure familiarity. When armored vehicles or remotely operated weapon systems are used in the defense, team leaders and operators should walk the engagement area so gunners can recognize dead spaces through their weapons sighting system.

(5) <u>Maximum Engagement Line (MEL).</u> The MEL is the depth of the sector and normally is limited to the maximum effective engagement range of the weapons systems. However, it can be less if there are objects or structures that prevent the security police officer from engaging targets at the maximum effective range of his assigned weapon. The distance to each MEL can be determined by a map reconnaissance or a terrain walk to ensure that the MELs are depicted accurately on the range card. Identifying an MEL may decrease ammunition expenditure by reducing attempts to engage the adversary at unreasonable distances.

(6) <u>Weapons Symbol, Left and Right Limits, and North Seeking Arrow.</u>

(a) The weapon symbols used in this example (Table 1) indicate the type of weapon (Figure 14 and Figure 15) for which that range card was designed.

Table 1. Weapon Symbols

Weapon System	Light	Medium	Heavy
Rifle/Automatic Weapon	↑	↟	↟
Anti-tank Gun	⏉	⊬	⊬
Rocket Launcher	⇑	⇑	⇑

Figure 14. .50 Caliber Sniper Rifle

Figure 15. Mk 19 Grenade Launcher

(b) The left and right limits of an SOF should be shown along with the terrain features or other recognizable objects, such as a building or other manmade structures used to mark those limits.

(c) Magnetic north should be shown on the card to aid in orienting the occupants relative to the position and to illustrate the relationship of the assigned SOF to the overall site defensive perimeter.

(7)   <u>Range Cards.</u> At least two copies of the range card (Figure 16) should be made for each position. One should remain in the position, and one should be placed in the command center. In the case of armored vehicles, each vehicle should contain a range card for every revetment or position that the vehicle is likely to occupy.

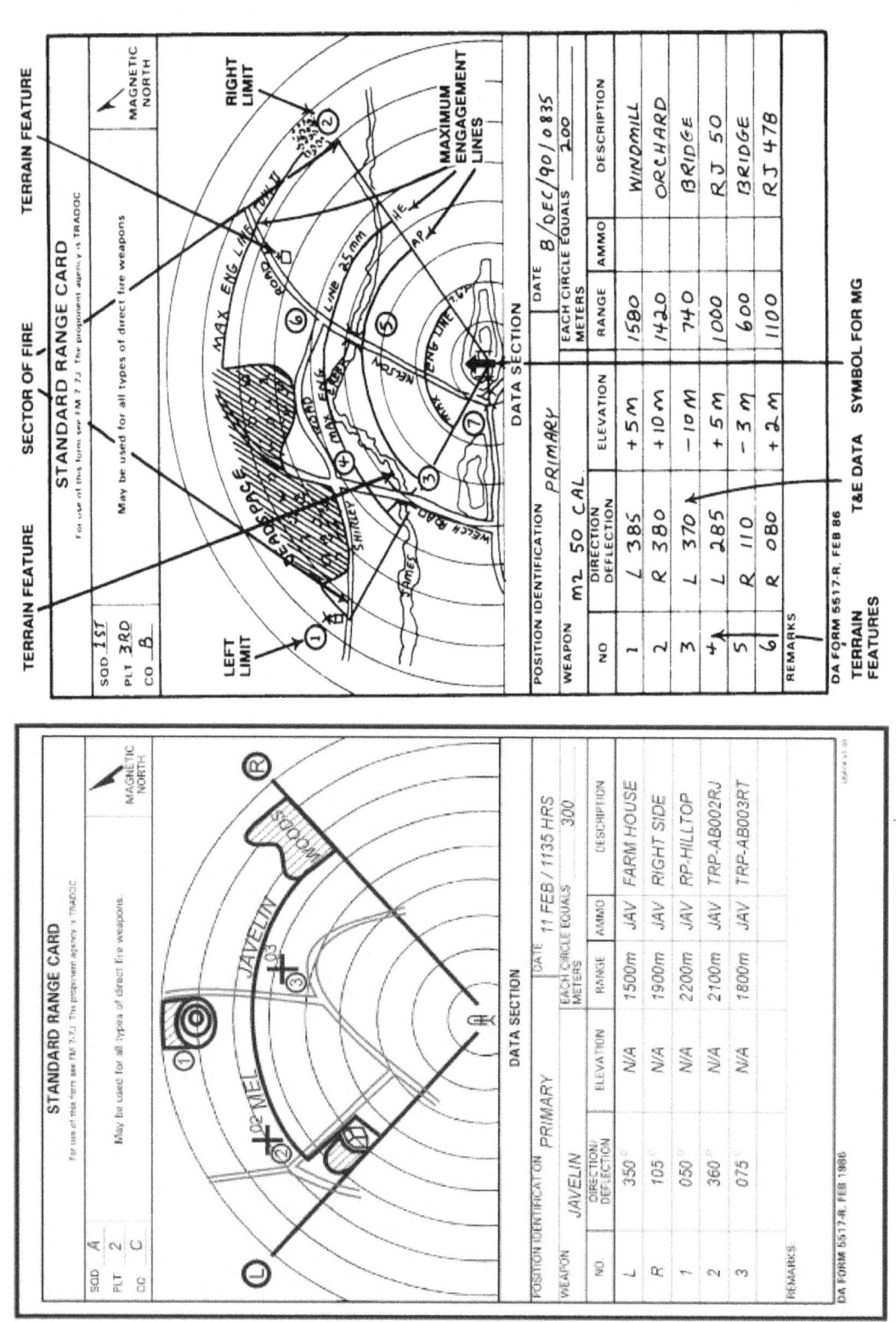

Figure 16. Sample Range Cards

29

e. Coordinating measures should be written clearly and precisely to reduce the potential for incidents of friendly fire casualties and to ensure that an adversary is neutralized as far from the target as possible.

    (1)   Occupants of each fixed fighting position should be aware of patrol or maneuver element activity within their SOF.

    (2)   A means should be established to track the locations of all patrol and tactical team movements relative to known reference points.

    (3)   Communications discipline should be strictly enforced at all times to ensure that all elements are continuously aware of the situation as the attack and response develop.

    (4)   Great care should be exercised to ensure that the communications system includes adequate alternate or backup capabilities and that positive visual signals are employed by maneuver elements when lifting supporting/suppressive fires for tactical teams to engage the adversary. Signaling schemes shall consider lighting and visibility conditions common to the site and operations.

3. SUMMARY.

a. The following minimum information should be depicted on defensive fire plan overlays and/or in narrative descriptions:

    (1)   Main terrain features in each sector;

    (2)   Location and types of obstacles and how they are covered by observation/fire;

    (3)   Dead space and how it is covered by observation/fire;

    (4)   Primary, alternate, and supplemental vehicle and tactical team positions;

    (5)   Crew-served weapons positions with primary and alternate directions of fire;

    (6)   Types of weapons in each position;

    (7)   Engagement area or primary and secondary SOFs for each position;

    (8)   Primary and alternate directions of fire for indirect fire weapons such as grenade launchers;

    (9)   Target reference points and patrol reference points in each sector;

    (10)   Observation post locations;

(11)   MELs for all weapon systems, including armored vehicles;

(12)   Indirect fire targets; and

(13)   Patrol routes.

b.   To ensure the effectiveness of the defensive fire plan, it should be validated by use of table-top exercises consisting of various scenarios, followed by limited scope performance testing and, ultimately, by full-scale force-on force performance testing.

c.   It cannot be emphasized too strongly that the defensive fire plan should follow, and be built upon, the barrier plan that has been developed from a detailed terrain analysis. All obstacles/barriers should be covered by either direct observation or by sensors and, when possible, by fire. SOFs for adjacent positions on the defensive perimeter shall, without exception, overlap/interlock to establish effective kill zones into which attackers are channeled by barriers, maneuver elements, or by fire, and every position should be able to support adjacent positions by fire (Figure 17).

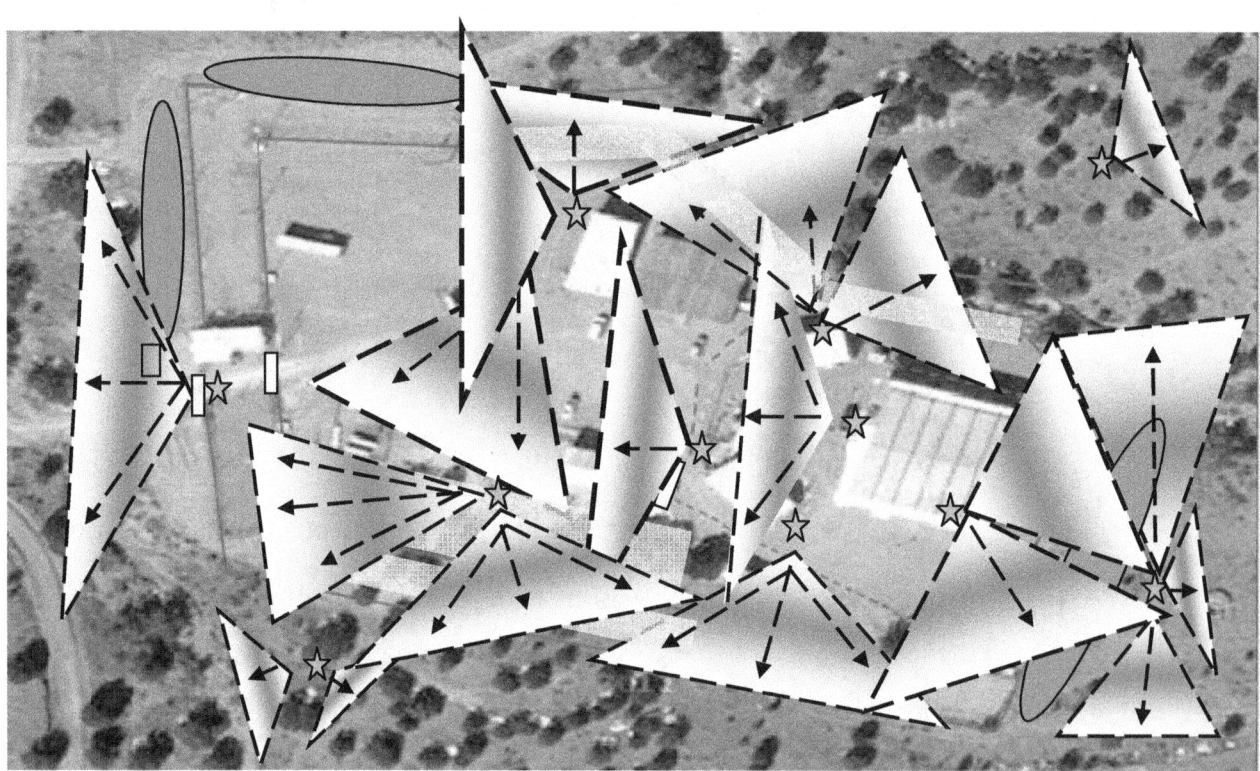

Figure 17. Layout with Interlocking Fields of Fire from Firing Positions, Interior and Exterior

APPENDIX D. DEFENSIVE PLANNING CHECKLIST

	CRITERIA	YES	NO	NA	COMMENTS
1.0	**Is the site/facility required to implement the Department of Energy tactical doctrine?**				
2.0	**Has a current vulnerability analysis been conducted?**				
3.0	**Has a current terrain analysis been completed?**				
3.1	Was a multidisciplinary team appointed and well briefed?				
3.2	Was site terrain evaluated in terms of its tactical applications:				
	• Observation and fields of fire?				
	• Cover and concealment?				
	• Obstacles?				
	• Key terrain?				
	• Avenues of approach?				
3.3	Were all lines of communication, drainage, buildings, and potential landing or drop zones identified and evaluated?				
3.4	Were the potential effects of climate and weather considered?				

	CRITERIA	YES	NO	NA	COMMENTS
3.5	Was intervisibility between/among fighting positions and the defensive perimeter evaluated?				
3.6	Were all dead spaces identified and evaluated?				
3.7	Was a formal report containing sketches, overlays, and explanatory notes prepared?				
4.0	**Has a current barrier plan been completed?**				
4.1	Was a multidisciplinary team appointed and well briefed?				
4.2	Was the barrier plan based on a current terrain analysis?				
4.3	Are all barriers covered by either direct or electronic observation and, when possible, by fire?				
4.4	Were barriers placed to channel attackers into preplanned kill zones of interlocking weapons fire?				
4.5	Was the current DOE O 473.3 consulted to ensure compliance with requirements for specific types of security areas?				
4.6	Did the team complete a terrain walk to ensure proper placement of obstacles/barriers?				
4.7	Was consideration given to the integration of remote electronic detection and assessment devices?				
4.8	Were barriers designed and constructed to enhance the ability of protective force (PF) tactical teams and/or armored vehicles to maneuver effectively?				

	CRITERIA	YES	NO	NA	COMMENTS
4.9	Are multiple layers of detection and delay employed and coupled with appropriate technologies to enhance PF capabilities?				
4.10	Do existing or proposed barriers provide protection for site targets and personnel from vehicle-borne or airborne improvised explosive devices?				
4.11	Was a formal report containing sketches, overlays, and explanatory notes prepared?				
4.12	Was the barrier plan validated using table-top exercises consisting of likely attack scenarios?				
5.0	**Has a current defensive fire plan been completed?**				
5.1	Was a team appointed consisting of those familiar with the site PF structure, weapons, equipment, tactical deployment, and maneuvering capabilities?				
5.2	Have hardened fighting positions been placed to take full advantage of natural and constructed obstacles and to provide maximum protection for PF personnel?				
5.3	Are all likely avenues of approach covered by observation and fire?				
5.4	Are all fighting positions mutually supporting?				
5.5	Do all fighting positions, fixed and hardened or supplemental, and armored vehicle response revetments have assigned primary sectors of fire that overlap those of adjacent positions on both sides around the entire defensive perimeter?				

	CRITERIA	YES	NO	NA	COMMENTS
5.6	Have all dead spaces in each sector been identified and addressed?				
5.7	Have maximum engagement lines for every weapon that may be deployed at each position been determined?				
5.8	Have range cards been produced for each weapon system assigned to, or likely to be deployed from, every fighting position and armored vehicle revetment?				
5.9	Do the defensive fire plan overlays and/or narrative descriptions depict:				
	• Main terrain features?				
	• Locations and types of obstacles?				
	• Dead spaces?				
	• Primary, alternate, and supplemental vehicle and tactical team positions?				
	• Crew served weapon positions with primary and alternate directions of fire?				
	• Types of weapons in each position?				
	• Engagement area or primary and secondary sectors of fire for each position?				
	• Primary and alternate directions of fire for indirect fire weapons?				
	• Target and patrol reference points in each sector?				
	• Observation post locations?				

CRITERIA	YES	NO	NA	COMMENTS
• Maximum engagement lines for all weapon systems, including armored vehicles?				
• Indirect fire targets?				
• Patrol routes?				
6.0	**Have tactical response plans been developed in support of the site/facility defensive plan?**				
6.1	Does the site have a secure command center possessing both primary and alternate means of communication with fixed and maneuver elements of the PF?				
6.2	Does the PF have a well defined command structure from the on-site commander down to the individual tactical team leaders?				
6.3	Do safeguards and security performance assurance plans address a means to assess the effectiveness of command and control systems and the ability of the PF to react should any of those systems be neutralized?				
6.4	Have all credible tactical scenarios been considered?				
6.5	Does the PF tactical response consist of teams of two or more security police officers?				
6.6	If a site employs single person patrols or posts, have specific rally points been selected so that tactical teams can be reconstituted prior to engaging the adversary?				
6.7	Has one leader been designated for each team?				

	CRITERIA	YES	NO	NA	COMMENTS
6.8	Are tactical response teams positioned on, or in close proximity to, target locations?				
6.9	If likely vertical insertion points cannot be covered adequately by fixed fighting positions surrounding the target, do response plans direct responding security police officers to move to preplanned positions that have good observation of those insertion points along with clear fields of fire?				
6.10	Do security incident response plans address security incidents, adversary intrusion of a facility/site, and defense against adversary use of weapons, explosives, and chemical/biological weapons as described DOE O 470.3B?				
6.11	Do response plans address maintaining a PF special response team of highly skilled security police officers with advanced training as a reserve element that can constitute a re-entry/recapture capability in addition to what is required to defend the facility adequately?				
6.12	Do security incident response plans provide specific response directions and required actions to PF personnel for applicable containment, denial, recapture, recovery, and pursuit strategies?				
6.13	Do security incident response plans provide specific response directions and required actions to PF personnel to support interruption/neutralization operations before completion of adversary task times?				

	CRITERIA	YES	NO	NA	COMMENTS
6.14	When a vulnerability assessment performance test and/or site security plan dictates a recapture strategy, do PF personnel have the ability to gain entry to the target facility?				
6.15	Does the defensive plan contain target-specific tactics, techniques, procedures, and equipment needed to perform the mission of recapturing an asset if it falls into adversary hands?				
6.16	Do PF tactical plans and training support a pursuit/recovery capability?				
6.17	Have security incident response plans been coordinated with site/facility emergency response plans?				
6.18	Do PF tactical response plans include primary and alternate devices or procedures to ensure the positive identification of friendly forces?				
6.19	Was due consideration given to the key aspects of the defensive plan that are essential to the success of the PF, including:				
	• Multiple layers of detection, beginning as far from the target as terrain and technology allow?				
	• A viable means of assessing adversary capabilities that may include closed circuit television, radar, sonic systems, and/or active patrolling by exterior forces?				
	• Multiple layers of delay along adversary approach routes, each covered by effective weapons fire?				

	CRITERIA	YES	NO	NA	COMMENTS
	• Carefully planned interlocking fields of fire from mutually supporting positions?				
	• Integration of mobile unit movements with defensive fire plans?				
	• Have any single point failures been identified addressed?				
6.20	Has consideration been given to the installation of active or passive denial systems on the target(s)?				
6.21	Have procedures been developed to ensure that site employees are trained on their responsibilities and actions in the event of an attack?				
6.22	Has consideration been given to how ammunition would be resupplied during a protracted firefight and to a means of evacuating wounded officers to medical facilities?				
6.23	Are current memoranda of agreement/memoranda of understanding maintained with local and Federal law enforcement agencies that address specific roles as well as how pursuit and recovery plans can be exercised?				
6.24	Do response plans address the potential for the involvement of hostages on or in proximity to the target(s)?				
6.25	Do response plans include site-specific tactics, techniques, and procedures for operating in a weapon of mass destruction environment?				
6.26	Have all security response plans been performance tested?				

39

CRITERIA		YES	NO	NA	COMMENTS
7.0	**Does the completed site defensive plan integrate all related elements into one document to make certain that no critical questions or issues are left unanswered and that each aspect has been cross-referenced to ensure adequate coordination has been accomplished?**				
7.1	Have all related documents been reviewed for classification?				
7.2	Have all related documents been appropriately marked?				
8.0	**Has a fully integrated force-on-force performance test of the site defensive plan been conducted?**				

INDEX

470.3B   1, 4, 34
470.4B   1, 4, 9, 14

A

acronyms   iii, 2
administrative escorts   11
adversarial incursion   3, 11, 20
adversary   2-9, 11-17, 20-1, 23, 25, 27, 33
  attack   4, 7-8
  avenues   24
  capabilities   10, 23, 35
  channel   15
  incursion   21
  intrusion   34
  maneuvering   21
  movement   17
  penetration   9
  task times   34
airborne   8, 21, 31
alarms, remote   9
analysis
  adversary threat   4
  current terrain   29-30
  current vulnerability   29
analytical tools   16
approach routes   5
  adversary   10, 35
  covered   17
area defense   4
armored vehicles   8, 12, 15, 22, 24-5, 27, 30, 33
assessment   4, 8-9
  checklist   1
attack axis   20
attrition areas   7, 15
automatic weapons   15
Avenues of Approach   17

B

barrier
  activated   10
  design   20-1
    effective   8
  requirements   20
  sound   6
barrier plan   7-10, 16, 19-23, 28, 30-1
  current   30
  strong   6
Barrier Planning   iii, 6, 20, 23
barriers/obstacles   8, 12, 23

C

chokepoints   12
climate   16-17, 29
closed circuit television   10, 35
command   13
  adversary's   21
  effective   12-13
command structure   13
  defined   13, 33
communications discipline   27
compensatory measures   18
Concealed   17
concealment   3, 17, 20, 29
concentric arrangement   4
concept, tactical   15
configuration   18
constitution/reconstitution   11
containment   1, 13
  applicable   34
  rapid   13
Containment Missions   3
coordination   9, 37
  close   24
Crew-Served Weapon System   iv, 9
Crew-served weapons   8, 19, 27

CONCLUDING MATERIAL

Review Activity
EM
Policy (HS-51)
HSS
MA
NE
NNSA
SC

Field and Operations Offices
CH
ID
NNSA Service Center
ORO
RL
SRO

Site Offices
ANL
INL
LASO
LLSO
NSO
OR
PSO
RLSO
SRSO
SSO
YSO

External Agency

Preparing Activity
Office of Security Policy (HS-51)

Project Number
SANS-0008